The heart-traveller

5

Sri Chinmoy

Flower-Flames

Ganapati Press

© 2021 SRI CHINMOY CENTRE

ISBN 978-1-911319-33-7

Cover drawing: Soul-bird by Sri Chinmoy

31 MARCH 2021

Flower-Flames

AUTHOR'S PREFACE

I have selected 207 poems out of 10,000 from my series, *Ten thousand Flower-Flames*, which was originally published in 100 volumes. Here the poet in me is soulfully satisfied, the reader in me is smilingly satisfied and the critic in me is surprisingly satisfied.

My Beloved Supreme, what more can I tell You, and what more do You expect from me?

"Be quiet, My poet-reader-critic-son. The Hour, My Hour, is about to strike."

—Sri Chinmoy

1. YOU HAVE DISCOVERED

My Lord,
I came to You with empty hands,
But You have discovered
My empty heart, too.

2. I CAME FROM GOD

I came from God
The Eternal Dreamer.
I am heading towards God
The Immortal Lover.

3. YOUR HAPPINESS-GIFT

Of all the gifts
I have offered to God,
My happiness-gift
He treasures most.

4. THE MIND WANTS TO INVENT

The mind wants to invent
A new God.
The heart wants to discover
The ancient and eternal God.

5. PLEASE WARN ME

My Lord,
Please warn me before You come.
Otherwise, You may come
　　unrecognised
And go back unloved.

6. MY HEART SAYS TO MY MIND

My mind says to my heart:
"Will you please praise God for me?"
My heart says to my mind:
"Will you please pray to God
To bless me?"

7. THE FARE

What is the fare
From earth to Heaven?
The fragrance-beauty
Of a gratitude-heart.

8. EVERY TIME I RUN AWAY FROM YOU

Every time I run away from You
And come back,
I see Your Eyes
More illumining than before,
And I feel Your Heart
More forgiving than before.

9. THE LORD OF MY THOUGHTS

My Lord, I am happy
Because You are the Lord of my life.
Can You not make me perfect
By becoming the Lord of my
　　thoughts?

10. TWO MIRACLES

The miracle of my sound-life:
It can chase God.

The miracle of my silence-life:
It can embrace God.

11. TWO SECRET WISHES

Two
Are my secret wishes:
I shall show God
Man's transformation-head.
I shall show man
God's Compassion-Feet.

12. NOT BEYOND POSSIBILITY

Not beyond man's possibility
Is God-realisation.
Not beyond earth's possibility
Is earth-transformation.
Not beyond my possibility
Is self-transcendence.

13. I DO NOT INTERFERE

I do not interfere in God's Affairs.
Every day I let Him
Create a new world.
God does not interfere in my affairs
Either.
Every day He lets me
Destroy an old world.

14. A NEW PRAYER

Your old prayer may not change
    God.
But God can grant you
A new prayer,
And this new prayer
Will make you really happy.
What is your new prayer?
God-Satisfaction
In God's own Way.

15. TO FRIGHTEN AND ENLIGHTEN

To frighten the animal in me
My God is all Justice.

To enlighten the human in me
My God is all Compassion.

16. GOD'S LION-POWER

Yesterday
I desired to be
God's Lion-Power.

Today
I desire to be
God's Deer-Speed.

Tomorrow
I shall desire to be
God's Lamb-Fondness.

17. WHAT YOU DID

God wanted you
To go to Him untouched.
But what you did,
You know!
You went to God unchanged!

18. ARE YOU TIRED, O LORD?

Are You, O Lord,
Tired of being good?
It seems You are.

Are You, O Lord,
Tired of being divine?
It seems You are.

Are You, O Lord,
Tired of being perfect?
It seems You are.

O my Lord Supreme,
Then do bless me
With Your Goodness-Heart,
Divinity-Life and Perfection-Role.

19. TWO OBSERVERS

God watched me from the sky
With His unchanging Compassion.
I watched God from the ground
With my increasing hesitation.

20. The boon

Scold me, my Lord, untiringly.
Insult me, my Lord, unreservedly.
But, my Lord, do not forget Your
    Boon.
You told me millions of years ago
That You would grant me
    the capacity
To love You sleeplessly.
Something more, unconditionally.

21. THE GOD-HOUR STRIKES

An unfinished Dream of God
Brought me down.
The God-Hour then struck.

An unending Reality of God
Will take me up.
The God-Hour will once again
    strike.

22. EVEN MY SHADOW AVOIDS ME

Even my shadow avoids me.
Even my body dislikes me.
Even my life disappoints me.
Even my God forgets me.

23. THE VERY LAST STEP

A heart of gratitude
Is the next-to-last step
Before we reach Heaven.

A life of surrender
Is the very last step
Before we reach Heaven.

24. MISTAKING EARTH FOR HEAVEN

Mistaking earth for Heaven,
He sighed.

Mistaking Heaven for earth,
He died.

25. CAN THIS BE TRUE?

Can this be true?
No desire binds me,
No temptation haunts me,
No imperfection blights me.
Can this be true?

26. DON'T TAKE A LATE START

Don't take a late start.
You may lose the race altogether.
Keep your love-devotion-surrender
Always on the alert.
Then you cannot have a late start.

27. O DESCENDING BLUE

O descending Blue,
I love you.

O ascending Green,
I love you.

O spreading Gold,
I love you.

28. ASPIRATION TELLS ME

Aspiration tells me
That my God is
Compassion-Mother.

Realisation tells me
That my God is
Liberation-Father.

Manifestation tells me
That my God is
Perfection-Friend.

29. A TINY ISLAND

God alone knows
When the Kingdom of Heaven
Will finally descend on earth.
In the meantime,
God is begging His aspiring children
To try to create
At least a tiny island
Which He can call Heaven on earth.

30. WHAT HAS GOD GIVEN ME?

What has God given me?
A beautiful heart.
What shall I give Him?
A soulful face.

31. THE TWENTIETH CENTURY

The twentieth century
Is flooded
With self-styled Master-rogues.

The twentieth century
Is flooded
With monster disciple-fools.

32. A WEEPING GOD

A thinking mind
Is a sinking life.

A sinking life
Is a dying promise.

A dying promise
Is a weeping God.

33. AN INTERESTING QUESTION

An interesting question:
Where is God?

An inspiring question:
What is God doing?

An illumining question:
Who is God?

A fulfilling question:
Who else's love do I need,
If not God's alone?

34. WHETHER YOU LIKE IT OR NOT

My Lord Supreme,
Whether You like it or not,
I shall come to You daily.
Whether You like it or not,
I shall tease You smilingly.
Whether You like it or not,
I shall place You on my shoulders
    surprisingly.

35. A GOOD PLACE

A good place to begin:
My soul's soulful nest.

A good place to continue:
My heart's psychic core.

A good place to transform:
My mind's mental factory.

36. SCIENCE IS

Indeed,
Science is man's
Breath-taking advance.

Indeed,
Spirituality is God's
Breath-immortalising romance.

37. MUSIC IS

Music is entertainment.
Music is enlightenment.
Music is the animal bark
Of man.
Music is the God-Song
And God-Dance for man.

38. FOUR ELEVATORS

Doubt-elevator never works.
Fear-elevator seldom works.
Confidence-elevator occasionally works.
Aspiration-elevator sleeplessly works.

39. HOW COULD THIS BE TRUE?

My Lord Supreme,
You rang my alarm clock.
How could this be true?
You prayed for my salvation.
How could this be true?
You concentrated on my
   illumination.
How could this be true?
You meditated for my realisation.
How could this be true?
You contemplated on my perfection.
How could this be true?
You lived for my satisfaction.
How could this be true?

40. PRAY FOR ME, PLEASE!

Heaven, pray for me, please!
I need the dream
Of oneness-perfection.

Earth, pray for me, please!
I need the reality
Of fulness-satisfaction.

41. TWO SUPREME SECRETS

My Lord told me a supreme secret:
"My child, I shall never scold you
    any more."
I told my Lord a supreme secret:
"My Father-Friend, I shall never
Disappoint You any more."

42. GOD IS MY COACH

God is my outer Coach.
Therefore, I smile and smile
After I succeed.

God is my inner Coach.
Therefore, I dance and dance
Before I proceed.

43. I HAVE TWO SERIOUS FAULTS

I have two serious faults:
I underestimate
God's Compassion-Beauty.
I overestimate
Man's ingratitude-reality.

44. I ENTERTAIN GOD

I entertain God
With my promise-power.
God entertains me
With His Compassion-shower.

45. I CHOSE

I chose not to understand God.
I chose not to understand even man.
But alas,
I chose to understand my
    clever mind.

46. YESTERDAY'S GOD

Yesterday's God
Belonged to my confidence.
Today's God
Belongs to my promise.
Tomorrow's God
Shall belong to my hope.

47. BY WAY OF JOKE

God gave me
By way of joke
A little mind.

I am giving God
In dead earnest
A big problem:
My useless life.

48. LET ME HELP YOU

My sweet Supreme Lord,
You have helped me
By speaking to me.
Let me help You
By listening to You.

49. I AM CHOOSING GOD'S LIGHT

Yesterday
I quickly chose God's Power
To fulfil me.

Today
I am quietly choosing God's Light
To illumine me.

50. MY PRAYER-WINGS CARRY ME

My prayer-wings
Carry me up to Heaven
To see God's Beauty.

My meditation-wings
Carry God down to earth
To see my heart's purity.

51. GOD'S FORGIVENESS FINDS ME

God's Forgiveness finds me
No matter where I am.
God's Compassion takes me
Where I ought to go.

52. I THINK OF GOD

I think of God
Because
I need God's Power.

God thinks of me
Because
He needs my love.

53. I APPEARED BEFORE GOD

I appeared before God
With what I have:
An iota of gratitude.

God appeared before me
With what He is:
Infinity's Satisfaction-Smile.

54. BECAUSE GOD LOVES ME MORE

Precisely because
God loves me infinitely more
Than I love myself,
God cannot afford to be
As careless with my life
As I am.

55. WHEN I PRAY TO THE FALSE GOD

When I pray
To the false God,
My praying is not enough.
I have to run towards him.
When I pray
To the real God,
He immediately runs towards me.

56. OLD GOD, NEW GOD

The old God
Taught me how to fight
Against ignorance-night.

The new God
Is teaching me how to surrender
To His Vision-Light.

57. PUZZLES

God's Greatness and Goodness
Puzzle me.
My weakness and meanness
Puzzle God.

58. I AM NOT NEEDED

I am not needed
To say the right thing.
I am only required
To be the right thing.

59. EACH HEART IS THE BEAUTY

Each heart is the beauty
Of a God-dreamer.
Each life is the delight
Of a God-lover.

60. EACH LISTENING HEART

Each listening heart
Is not a bud of infancy.
Each listening heart
Is a flower of God-Ecstasy.

61. DO NOT WASTE TIME

Do not waste time.
Time is precious.
Do not exploit God.
God is gracious.
Do not mix with ignorance.
Ignorance is ferocious.
Do not play with doubt.
Doubt is injurious.
Do not cherish insecurity.
Insecurity is infectious.
Do not harbour impurity.
Impurity is dangerous.

62. IF I CAN SEE GOD'S FACE

If I can see God's Face
Even once,
I am sure He will make
Some room for me
To stay in His Heart
As long as I want to.

63. SELF-IMPRISONMENT BEGINS

Self-imprisonment begins
The day we start playing
With expectation-snare,
And not before.

64. MY HEART REPRESENTS

My heart represents
God the Duty
On earth.

My soul represents
God the Beauty
In Heaven.

65. PEACE NEEDS NO INTERPRETATION

Peace needs no interpretation.
Love needs no explanation.
Oneness needs no expression.

66. THREE ULTIMATE ABSURDITIES

Three ultimate absurdities:
I shall fail my Lord.
I am not meant for God-realisation.
My Lord is not pleased with me.

67. GOD'S TROUBLES

God's troubles are these:
The animal in man
Has forgotten Him totally.
The divine in man
Is not manifesting Him
    satisfactorily.

68. WE ARE MISTAKEN

You are mistaken.
God does think of you constantly.
I am mistaken.
God does love us both equally.

69. A DREAMER OF GOD-DREAMS

Unless I become a sleepless dreamer
Of God-dreams,
My heart shall remain a fount
Of orphan-tears.

70. I KNOW WHOSE I AM

True,
I do not know
Who I am,
But I do know
Whose I am.

71. MIRACLES WORTH SEEING

Only two miracles are worth seeing:
The miracle of loving
And
The miracle of forgiving.

72. HEAVEN KNOWS HOW TO LIBERATE

Darkness knows how to thicken.
Light knows how to brighten.
Earth knows how to bind
The divine in man.
Heaven knows how to liberate
The human from the animal.

73. CENTURIES HAVE ROLLED AWAY

Centuries have rolled away,
And still the outer man does not
　　know
Where the inner man
Unmistakably is,
And the inner man does not know
What the outer man
Actually wants.

74. A GOD-DREAMER AND A GOD-LOVER

The difference
Between a God-dreamer
And a God-lover
Is this:
A God-dreamer wants to live
In God's birthless and deathless
    Infinity;
A God-lover longs to live
In God's Heart-Cave.

75. MANY WAYS

No way
To persuade God.
No way
To deceive God.
But many ways
Not only to realise God
But also to become God.

76. WHEN I PRAY

When I pray,
I pray for the right thing:
Peace.

When I meditate,
I meditate on the right Person:
God.

77. MY HEART'S CONSTANT GUEST

My heart's constant guest:
God the Many.
My life's constant host:
God the One.

78. I MEASURED MY SUCCESS

Yesterday
I measured my success
By competing with others.

Today
I measure my success
By competing with myself.

Tomorrow
I shall measure my success
By expanding my heart
To encompass others.

79. TWO LINES TO HEAVEN

The soulful meditation-line
    to Heaven
Is never busy
Because
Very few seekers have the capacity
To use that line.

The wild frustration-line to Heaven
Is always busy
Because
Everybody has the capacity
To use that line.

80. INTENTION AND CAPACITY

Hope has no real intention
Of deceiving us.
Alas, it has no adequate capacity
To please us.

81. ACCEPTED BY TRUTH

You are accepted
By Truth.
That means you are liberated
By God.

82. TWO THINGS I MUST NEVER FORGET

Two things I must never forget:
My meditation-appointment with
    God
In the small hours of the morning,
And God's Satisfaction-appointment
    with me
In the late hours of the night.

83. THEY WILL DO IT FOR YOU

Do not blame yourself.
This world will do it for you,
Far beyond your imagination.

Do not admire yourself.
The higher worlds will do it for you,
Far beyond your expectation.

84. HIS LIFE'S EARLY MORNING

His life's early morning
Saw God's Forgiveness-Feet.
His life's late evening
Shall see God's Compassion-Eye.

85. ALLOW GOD TO BECOME REAL

You are bound to know
God's Will
If you allow God
To become real to you.

86. THREE HIMALAYAN PRAYERS

Three Himalayan prayers:
Lord, do give me the capacity
To love Your Forgiveness-Feet
Unreservedly.
Lord, do give me the capacity
To love Your Compassion-Heart
Untiringly.
Lord, do give me the capacity
To love Your Justice-Eye
Unconditionally.

87. ONLY A FOOL

Only a fool
Thinks that he is independent.
Only a fool
Feels that he is indispensable.

88. SWEET IS MY LORD

Sweet is my Lord
Because He is knowable.
Sweeter is my Lord
Because He is known.
Sweetest is my Lord
Because He invites me
To play hide-and-seek with Him
Every day.

89. BE AWARE!

Be aware!
God definitely exists.
Be awake!
God will come and knock
At your door.

90. IF IT IS TRUE

If it is true
That Jesus is coming again,
Then it is also true
That you and I should go to meet
Him
And welcome Him
At the halfway point.

91. BECAUSE I LOVE GOD

Because I fear God,
I do not have to fear any man.
Because I love God,
I have to love all human beings.

92. GOD NEEDS ME

God loves me.
I mean,
My sincere cry.

God wants me.
I mean,
My simple life.

God needs me.
I mean,
My pure heart.

93. ONE DESIRE AND ONE ASPIRATION

O my Supreme Lord,
I have only one desire:
Do give me the thing
That pleases me for a fleeting day.

O my Supreme Lord,
I have only one aspiration:
Do give me the thing
That pleases You forever and forever.

94. AN UNFINISHED MAN

Because of his shallow mind
He is an unfinished man.

Because of his vast heart
He is in unextinguished pain.

95. I HAVE LOST YOU

I have lost You, My Lord,
Not because my intimate friend
Is tenebrous ignorance-night,
But because I have never dared to
    claim You
As my own, very own.

96. MY LIFE NEEDS GUIDANCE

Attention—
My body needs attention.

Encouragement—
My vital needs encouragement.

Inspiration—
My mind needs inspiration.

Aspiration—
My heart needs aspiration.

Guidance—
My life needs guidance.

97. LIVE ONLY FOR GOD'S LOVE

You do not have to prove
God's Love for you.
Just feel that you live
Only for God's Love.

98. GOD COMPASSIONATELY ASKS

God compassionately asks me,
"Will you be available?"
He never asks me,
"Will you be able?"

99. ONLY ONE INNER TEACHER

I have only one inner teacher:
A gratitude-flame.
I have only one outer teacher:
A surrender-drop.

100. ONLY THE CHOSEN

Everybody can begin,
But only the chosen
Can divinely continue
And supremely succeed.

101. TO BE IN GOD'S COMPANY

If you do not have
A sense of humour,
Then God will not choose you
To be in His close company.

102. AN ARMOUR OF PROOF

What my mind wants
Is a strong armour of proof.
What my heart needs
Is a sweet ripple of belief.

103. THE RETURN-JOURNEY

Greatness is a matter
Of a moment.
Goodness is the work
Of a lifetime.
Oneness is the return-journey
Of birth and death.

104. DREAMERS AND LOVERS

As a dreamer,
You are loved by God
Constantly.

As a Lover,
God is loved by you
Unconditionally.

105. ONE IDOL, ONE HERO

I have only one idol,
And that idol is my crying heart.
I have only one hero,
And that hero is my smiling soul.

106. GOD GAVE ME HIS HEART

Something new happened
This morning:
I came to realise
That God still loves me.

Something new happened
This evening:
God gave me His Heart
And took away my mind
In exchange.

107. PHILOSOPHY EMBODIES

Philosophy embodies
God-information.
Religion embodies
God-aspiration.
Spirituality embodies
God-Satisfaction.

108. MY MIND TELLS ME

In the morning
My mind tells me:
"Young man,
You are supremely useful."

In the evening
My mind tells me:
"Old man,
You are absolutely useless."

109. TAKE THE TEMPEST OUT

My Lord,
Do take my mind
Out of the tempest.
"My child,
Let Me first take the tempest
Out of your mind."

110. TWO SUPREME REALITIES

Do not descend from Heaven
After me.
My heart will feel miserable.

Do not descend from Heaven
Before me.
Your soul will not appreciate it.

God has two supreme Realities:
Togetherness-life
And
Oneness-heart.

111. MY SEARCH ENDS

In the morning
My search for realisation ends
Inside my Lord's Compassion-Heart.

At noon
My search for perfection ends
Inside my Lord's Vision-Eye.

In the evening
My search for satisfaction ends
At my Lord's Beauty-Feet.

112. TODAY I AM WISE

Yesterday I was clever.
That is why
I wanted to change the world.

Today I am wise.
That is why
I am changing myself.

113. THE BEGINNING

Self-observation is the beginning
Of self-perfection.
Self-perfection is the beginning
Of God-Satisfaction.
God-Satisfaction is the beginning
Of God's new Dream.

114. A "NO" FROM YOUR HEART

One thing you must know:
A "no" from your heart
Is infinitely stronger
Than all the hostile forces in the
 world.

115. SOMETHING SPECIAL

God gave me something special:
Awareness.
I gave God something special:
Willingness.
Now God wants to give me
His Satisfaction
And I want to give God
My gratitude.

116. A TIME WHEN YOU DO NOT LOVE ME

My Lord, do You love me
Even when I kill time?
"Yes, My child, I love you."
My Lord, is there any time
When You do not love me?
"Yes, My child, there is a time
When I do not love you."
When, my Lord, when?
"When you think that you are not
A budding God."

117. SELF-MASTERY AND GOD-DISCOVERY

Self-mastery and God-discovery
Are the only two things
That each human being on earth
Must take seriously.
Everything else can be taken lightly.

118. THE SUPREME FULFILLER

My body,
I have been helping you
For such a long time.
Nevertheless, you are an idler.

My vital,
I have been helping you
For such a long time.
Nevertheless, you are an aggressor.

My mind,
I have been helping you
For such a long time.
Nevertheless, you are a doubter.

My heart,
I have been helping you
Since this morning.
I clearly see that you are a born
　　lover.

My soul,
I have just started serving you.
To my extreme joy I find
That you are the supreme fulfiller.

119. BEFORE YOUR MIND TELLS YOU

Every day, before your mind
    tells you
That it has something special
To give to the world,
Let your heart tell you
That it has something special
To receive from Heaven.

120. THREE ALTERNATIVES

Remember, O my mind,
You have three alternatives:
You can either go
From darkness to light
Or from light to darkness,
Or you can remain where you are:
In your self-created unawareness.

121. GOD HAS THE SINCERITY

God has the sincerity
To tell me
That He loves me.
Alas, I do not have the sincerity
To tell Him
That I badly need His Love.

122. BEFORE I REACH YOU

My Lord Supreme,
Do grant me a boon:
Before I reach You,
Do allow my gratitude-heart
To precede me.

123. I AFFIRM WHAT GOD AFFIRMS

I affirm what God affirms.
What does God affirm?
He affirms that God-realisation
Is my birthright.

I negate what God negates.
What does God negate?
He negates that I am a member
Of ignorance-society.

124. SILENCE AND FULFIL

Silence
Your endless earth-necessity
Secretly.

Fulfil
Your breathless Heaven-necessity
Immediately.

125. MAN CRAWLS TOWARDS GOD

The difference between
Man and God is this:
Man unknowingly
Crawls towards God;
God compassionately
Runs towards man.
Man thinks that he has God;
God knows that man is God.

126. I BOW

I sleeplessly bow to the Light
That never dims.
I breathlessly bow to the Delight
That never fades.

127. MY BELOVED SUPREME IS SEARCHING

My Beloved Supreme is searching
For my willingness
And not for my capacity.

My Beloved Supreme is searching
For my readiness
And not for my perfection.

128. REMEMBER WHAT YOU SAID

Remember what you said to God:
"My Lord, I shall always
Fulfil You unconditionally."

Remember what you said to man:
"My friend, I shall always
Help you unreservedly."

129. YOU ARE LONELY BECAUSE

You want to know why you
　　are lonely?
You are lonely because
You never want to hear
Your heart's oneness-song.

130. THE SAVIOUR TEACHES ME

The Scriptures teach me
How to love the Saviour.
The Saviour teaches me
How to love the Real in me,
The future God.

131. GOD THE YOUNG AND GOD THE OLD

I love
Both God the young
And God the old.

From God the young I learn
How to run, jump, fly and dive.

From God the old I learn
How to cry and smile
And how to smile and cry.

132. YOU COME TO REALISE

When you pray,
You come to realise
That you have a room high above.

When you meditate,
You come to realise
That you have a home deep inside.

133. AN UNCONDITIONAL LIFE

In the beginning
An unconditional life
Is a battlefield.
But eventually
An unconditional life
Becomes a playground.

134. A TRUE AND SLEEPLESS LOVE OF GOD

If you have a true and sleepless
Love of God,
Then nobody will be able to snatch
 you away
From the Embrace of God.

135. A GOD-LOVER KNOWS

A God-seeker thinks
That he can be free.
A God-server feels
That he will be free.
A God-lover knows
That he is free.

136. I SHALL FORGIVE AND FORGET

I shall forgive and I shall forget.
I shall forgive my past unwillingness
To meditate on God.
I shall totally forget
My very, very old friend:
Ignorance.

137. DO YOU NOT REMEMBER?

Do you not remember
That only the other day
You loved God unconditionally?

Do you not remember
That only the other day
You claimed God as your own,
    very own?

138. EVERY DAY MY HEART TURNS

Every day my mind turns
Towards the miracle-working God.
Every day my heart turns
Towards the life-illumining God.

139. I SHALL OBEY YOU UNCONDITIONALLY

My Lord,
I shall obey You unconditionally
Provided You tell me
That I am Your best student.
"My child,
I shall tell the world
You are My best student
Provided I am your only Teacher
And you completely give up
 your other teacher:
Ignorance."

140. GOD CAME DOWN

I went up
To see God's beautiful Feet.
God came down
To give me His bountiful Heart.

141. DO YOU LOVE ME, MY LORD?

Do You love me, my Lord,
No matter what I say
And no matter what I do against
  You?

"Tell Me first, My son,
Do you need Me
No matter how strict I am with
  you?"

142. WHEN I USE WHAT I HAVE

When I use what I have:
A commitment-lamp,
God gives me what He has:
His Contentment-Sun.

143. MY HEART LONGS TO WORK FOR GOD

The difference
Between my mind and my heart
Is this:
My mind wants to play with God.
My heart longs to work for God.

144. MY SUPREME MOMENT

This is my day;
I love it.

This is my morning God-Hour;
I need it.

This is my supreme moment;
I am it.

145. TWO PERSONS LOVE ME

Two persons love me:
Satan and God.
Satan loves me
So that he can use me
As his faithful slave.
God loves me
So that He can have me
As His cheerful friend.

146. HIS ANCIENT HEART TELLS HIM

My ancient heart tells me
That God is beautiful plus powerful.
My modern mind tells me
That God is either unmindful
    or doubtful.

147. TO BE CLOSER TO GOD

To be closer to God,
Be a better cry
And
Have a better smile.

148. NO PARTITION

There is neither a visible
Nor an invisible partition
Between self-giving
And God-becoming.

149. GO AND SEE GOD PERSONALLY

Be not afraid!
Take the first step.
Go and see God personally.
His Omnipotence will prove to you
That it is also His universal Love.

150. HE IS ETERNALLY PERFECT

You love God
Because He is supreme.
God loves you
Because you are His powerful
Dream.

You need God
Because He is eternally perfect.
God needs you
Because you are His choice Project.

151. BEFORE I CALL

Before I call,
God's Compassion-Eye answers.
Before I start,
God's Compassion-Heart
Finishes the race for me.

152. I DO HAVE THE CAPACITY

True, I do not have the capacity
To touch God's Compassion-Feet,
But I do have the capacity
To feel God's Forgiveness-Heart.

153. A SELF-WORSHIPPER

Do not say anything
To a self-worshipper,
For God knows how and why
He is stabbing his own heart.

154. DO NOT DIE UNSUNG

O my heart,
Do not die unsung.
O my mind,
Do not die unsettled.
O my vital,
Do not die unchallenged.
O my body,
Do not die untransformed.

155. WHEN HE REALISED GOD

When he realised God for himself,
God said to him,
"My son, I may use you
In the distant future."

When he realised God for others,
God said to him,
"My son, I shall use you
In the near future."

When he realised God for God,
God said to him,
"My son, I am using you
And I shall use you
Sleeplessly and eternally."

156. A SOULFUL SMILE

A soulful smile
Can kindle the universe.
A breathless cry
Can feed the universe.

157. DO NOT ASK FOR TOO LITTLE

Do not ask for too little.
When you do that,
God's Heart of Magnanimity
Is tearfully embarrassed.

158. A VERY SIMPLE QUESTION

God has asked a very simple
    question:
Do you want to be like Him?
He is eagerly waiting
For your open-hearted answer.

159. HIS WEIGHT IS AS LIGHT

My Lord Supreme,
Out of His infinite Bounty,
Tells me that His Weight is at once
As light as my heart's aspiration-cry
And as heavy as my life's
    ingratitude-frown.

160. YOU WANT TO SEE GOD'S FACE

You want to see God's Face
To satisfy yourself.
God wants to embrace your heart
To satisfy Himself.

161. EACH TIME I COMPROMISE

Each time I compromise
With ignorance-night,
I kill the beauty and purity
Of my climbing heart-plant.

162. GOD HAS OPENLY FED YOU

God has openly fed you
With His Compassion-Sea.
Will you not even secretly feed Him
With your heart's gratitude-drops?

163. MAN'S MODERN FRUITS

Man's ancient roots:
His cries and smiles.
Man's modern fruits:
His laughter and sighs.

164. ONLY ONE ANSWER

You have a multitude of questions,
But there is only one answer:
The road is right in front of you,
And the guide is waiting for you.

165. DO NOT SPEAK ILL OF YOURSELF

Do not speak ill of yourself.
The world around you
Will always gladly do that
On your behalf.

166. A SMILE CARRIES

An outer smile carries
Today's earthly dawn to Heaven.
An inner smile carries
Tomorrow's Heavenly sun to earth.

167. NEVER FORGET ONE THING

Never forget one thing:
The Ultimate Truth is your friend
And not your enemy.

168. TOTALLY MISTAKEN

I was totally mistaken
When I thought I loved God
Unconditionally.

I was completely mistaken
When I thought God did not
 need me
At all.

169. ONE THING TO LEARN

Every day there is only
One thing to learn:
How to be honestly happy.

170. TWO UNNECESSARY QUESTIONS

Two unnecessary questions:
Does God love me?
Do I need God?

171. GOD WANTS TO KNOW

God does not want to know
Why I cry,
But He does want to know
Why I do not smile.

172. HUNGER AND FEAST

What is success?
My expansion-hunger.
What is progress?
My perfection-feast.

173. THE SUPREME CONTRIBUTION

The great contribution
Of the human life:
Mind over matter.

The supreme contribution
Of the divine life:
Heart over mind.

174. ONLY TWO SUPERIOR WAYS

There are only two superior ways
To realise God:
My life's surrender-way
And my heart's gratitude-way.

175. SATISFACTION-LION AND ASPIRATION-DEER

Satisfaction-lion
Will have to postpone its
    momentous visit
Because aspiration-deer
Has not yet started its journey.

176. WHAT I CAN DO FOR GOD

I shall see
What I can do for God
Since I am not doing
Anything worthwhile for man.

177. A DIPLOMATIC DEATH

Since each thought
Is an atomic power,
You can give each thought
A diplomatic death.

178. TWO ANCIENT UNIVERSAL QUESTIONS

Two ancient universal questions:
How can I realise God
Immediately?
Is unconditional surrender
Ever possible?

179. AT LAST MY HEART HAS CHALLENGED

At last my heart
Has challenged my mind,
Not to defeat it
But to transform it.

180. ALWAYS AVAILABLE

God may not be always available,
But God's Compassion-Sea
And Forgiveness-Sky
Are always available.

181. TWO INHERITED DISASTERS

Two disasters he has inherited
From his many ignorance-lives:
A doubting mind
And
An unaspiring heart.

182. A GOD-CLIMBING HEART

What I need is
A God-climbing heart
And not
A God-manufacturing mind.

183. ONLY TWO REALITY-LOVERS

There are only two reality-lovers:
One is God
The Immortal Singer;
The other is God
The Eternal Listener.

184. ALTHOUGH GOD IS INFINITE

Although God is infinite,
He prefers to live
Inside man's tiny heart-nest.

185. GOD ASKS ME TO GIVE HIM

God asks me to give Him
The things that I myself
Do not at all care for:
My imperfections.

186. ETERNITY'S INFINITE QUESTIONS

Man has his Eternity's
Infinite questions.
God has His Immortality's
Only answer:
Oneness-embrace.

187. TWO FIRM CONVICTIONS

True, God has not given me
Everything,
But He has given me
Two firm convictions:
He loves me
No matter what I do;
I shall need Him
No matter what I become.

188. FAITH WILL CHANGE HIS FUTURE

Sincerity
Changed my past
Slowly and steadily.

Determination
Is changing my present
Powerfully and convincingly.

Faith
Will change my future
Amazingly and permanently.

189. GOD DOES NOT LAUGH

God does not laugh at our prayers,
No matter how insincere they are.
But God does laugh when we
    think and feel
That our prayers will never
    be answered.

190. MY DUBIOUS PRAYER-LIFE

My dubious prayer-life
May not satisfy God,
But my glowing surrender-heart
Will always satisfy God.

191. THE SONS OF MORNING SANG

The sons of morning sang
And reminded me of God the Power.
The daughters of evening sang
And reminded me of God of Peace.

192. GOD LOVES US

God loves us
Even after we have failed Him.
We need God
Even after we have realised Him.

193. GOD'S "WHY?" AND "HOW?"

I came from God
To learn the meaning
Of His "Why?"

I shall go back to God
After I have learnt the meaning
Of His "How?"

194. HIS ARE THE TEARS

Mine are not the tears
Of disappointed expectation.
Mine are the tears
Of unexpected inner joy.

195. COMPLETELY LOST

The world is completely lost
Between your manifested stupidity
And your unmanifested divinity.

196. ONLY ONE ANSWER

There are countless questions
About God,
But only one answer:
God is His own Eternity's
Satisfaction-distribution.

197. ASPIRATION WITHOUT DEDICATION

Aspiration without dedication
Is like a slow runner
Who knows where the goal is
But is bound to arrive shockingly
    late.

198. THE SACRED HEART OF THE MOON

The sacred heart of the moon
Comes from the secret
    Smile of God.
The sacred breath of the sun
Comes from the open Dance of God.

199. TWO UNANSWERED QUESTIONS

Two are the questions
That I do not know how to answer:
Does God actually need me?
What will happen
If I become another God?

200. SOMEDAY

Someday God will forgive me.
It may be soon.
Someday I shall satisfy God.
It may take a little time.

201. I NEED THREE THINGS DESPERATELY

I need three things desperately:
An ancient heart,
A modern arm
And an ultra modern-eye.

202. ONE WILLING BREATH

A willing breath
Sees the Face of God.
A surrendering life
Becomes the heart of God.

203. BECAUSE I AM A TRUTH-SEEKER

Because I am a truth-seeker
My future flows towards me.
Because I am a God-lover
I live in my Eternal Now.

204. TAKE YOUR CHOICE!

Take your choice!
Either allow God
To sit inside your head
Or go and sit
At God's Forgiveness-Feet.

205. TWO INCREDIBLE FACTS

Two incredible facts:
God was chasing away my
 desire-tiger.
My doubting mind was untiringly
Following God.

206. WRONG AND RIGHT PRAYERS

"God, give me!"
This is a wrong and improper prayer.
"God, take me!"
This is a right and proper prayer.

207. GOD THE LOVER

We pray to God the Power,
But God the Lover
Answers our prayers.

Notes

The 1985 printings of *Flower-Flames*.

Two printings of *Flower-Flames* are extant, both published by Agni Press on February 1985. One has Sri Chinmoy's painting of a rose on the cover, the other has a Jharna-Kala painting dated "September 1975". The printing with Jharna-Kala painting is slightly different.

This edition follows the 1985 edition with a painting of a rose.

APPENDIX

Bibliography

Sri Chinmoy:
— *Flower-Flames,* Agni Press, 1985

Table of contents

Flower-Flames
Flower-Flames 1

Appendix
Bibliography 136

Table of contents 138

The heart-traveller

1. Aspiration-Flames — Aspiration and God's Hour
2. A Sri Chinmoy primer
3. Everest-Aspiration
4. New Year's Messages from Sri Chinmoy (1966-2007)
5. Flower-Flames

www.ingramcontent.com/pod-product-compliance
Lightning Source LLC
Chambersburg PA
CBHW021440080526
44588CB00009B/609